BAINTE DEN STOC

WITHDRAWN FROM DLR LIBRARIES STOCK

KU-432-844

being a model

Adam Sutherland

First published in 2012 by Wayland

Copyright © Wayland 2012

Wayland
Hachette Children's Books
338 Euston Road
London NW1 3BH

Wayland Australia
Level 17/207 Kent Street
Sydney NSW 2000

All rights reserved

Concept by Joyce Bentley

Commissioned by Debbie Foy and
Rasha Elsaeed

Produced for Wayland by Calcium
Designer: Paul Myerscough
Editor: Sarah Eason

British Library Cataloguing in Publication Data

Being a model. — (Top jobs)(Radar)
    1. Models (Persons)—Juvenile literature.
    I. Title II. Series
    746.9'2'092-dc23

ISBN: 978 0 7502 6599 7

Every effort has been made to clear copyright.
Should there be any inadvertent omission, please
apply to the publisher for rectification.

Printed in China

Wayland is a division of Hachette Children's Books,
an Hachette UK company.

www.hachette.co.uk

Acknowledgements: Joy Fatoyinbo: 18–19, 18br,
19bc, 19br, back cover; Gemma Howorth: 2t, 9;
istock: Joel Carillet 15r; Shutterstock: Subbotina
Anna 30–31, Apollofoto 1, 14r, Jorge Cubells Biela
4–5, Cinemafestival 11b, Conrado 15tl, Olga
Ekaterincheva 25br, Helga Esteb 2b, 20, 21tr, 26,
Featureflash 24br, Ben Heys 6–7, Geoffrey Jones
3br, Monkey Business Images 25tr, Anton Oparin
1r, Lev Radin 15bl, Julian Ribinik 28–29, Stocklight
10–11, Mayer George Vladimirovich 3l, 24tr,
Debby Wong 2c, 22–23, Natalia Yeromina cover,
6, 17r, Serg Zastavkin 12–13.

The website addresses (URLs) included in this book were
valid at the time of going to press. However, because
of the nature of the internet, it is possible that some
addresses may have changed, or sites may have
changed or closed down since publication.

cover stories

8

REAL LIFE STORY
Discover how your hands, lips
or feet could be your fortune!

22

POSTER PAGE
Take a look at one of the
world's leading male models

24

BIG DEBATE
Should size zero be
banned from catwalks?

26

STAR STORY
The story of model and
actress Scarlett Johansson

Leabharlanna Dhún Laoghaire · Ráth An Dúin

thepeople

8   **REAL LIFE STORY** Star hands

10   **TOP FIVE** Most successful models

18   **5-MINUTE INTERVIEW** Joy Fatoyinbo

20   **READ ALL ABOUT IT** Hollywood models

22   **POSTER PAGE** Tyson Beckford

26   **STAR STORY** Scarlett Johansson

themoves

14   **ZONE IN** Working the look

28   **PICTURE THIS!** Front row

thetalk

4   **FEEL IT** Showtime!

6   **ALL ABOUT** Strike a pose!

12   **PULL A NUMBER** Vital statistics

16   **THE LINGO** Model speak

24   **BIG DEBATE** Size zero
on the catwalk – yes or no?

30   **RECORD BREAKERS**
Action figures

32   **FAN CLUB**
Walk this way!

32   **INDEX**

SHOWTIME!

You're out of bed before dawn and at the venue early, ready for the hours of preparation before the catwalk show. You are nervous but excited, you feel butterflies in your stomach. You're keen to impress. This is a big show for one of the top designers in the fashion industry. Someone you've always wanted to model for. You're determined to make a really good impression, and hopefully you'll be back on the catwalk for him next season, too.

VICTORIO & LUCCHINO

Get the look

You take your place in front of the mirror alongside a dozen other girls. Two hours of hair and make-up lie ahead. People are buzzing around you like autograph hunters around a pop star. While someone does your eyes, there is an assistant on your lips, and two more on your hair. Next come the outfits. You'll be modelling quite a few today, and quick changes are essential. The dressers are like a Formula One pit crew – everyone with his or her own job to do, working like a well-oiled machine. Even the most elaborate outfits are on and off in a matter of seconds.

Walk the walk

Here goes! You're in the first outfit – a floor-length skirt and towering heels – and it's time to hit the catwalk. No matter how many times you do this, you can't get used to it. It's a huge buzz – the adrenalin makes you light-headed. Your mouth is dry, your heart's trying to beat its way out of your chest. You take a deep breath and step onto the runway. In an instant, your training and experience take over. You move almost unconsciously through your routine – to the end of the catwalk, turn, pause and back.

Back for more

The show has gone brilliantly well. The audience has been applauding throughout. Now, at the close, it's like the end of a rock concert. The crowd is on its feet, cheering and calling for the designer. He grabs your hand, walks out onto the catwalk, and takes a bow. You're so proud, you're walking on air. It's a fantastic feeling. One you'll never forget.

Go and see

When models are not in front of a camera, they are often expected to attend castings or visit potential new clients or photographers. These visits are called 'go-sees'. They are the least glamorous part of the job. Models can spend an hour or more waiting for a two-minute meeting.

STRIKE A POSE!

For many young people, modelling looks like an incredible job. Wearing great clothes, travelling the world… and getting paid for it! But like most jobs, it involves a lot of hard work and dedication to reach the top. Modelling is made up of different people playing key roles. Here are some of them.

On the books

Models are represented by model agencies. The agency is responsible for finding a model work, negotiating their fees, introducing the model to new brands, photographers and magazines. The agency manages the model's career. Fashion models work with only one agency. Commercial models can be on two or three agencies' books.

Booked up

A model's diary is organised by a model booker. Depending on the size of the agency, there could be one or a dozen bookers working together. Each booker looks after a certain number of models, and builds up a strong working relationship with them. Fashion models contact their booker at the end of every working day to find out their diary for the following day. Commercial models are contacted by their agency if they are required to attend a casting for a particular job.

Finding faces

Scouting is very important. Fashion agencies send scouts to large events, such as music festivals, to search for new faces. Scouts are looking for 'the next big thing', the new Lily Cole or Kate Moss. They are often searching for something out of the ordinary, but they always want height. Women must be 175 centimetres or taller and men 183 centimetres or taller. Models must be even taller than this for catwalk work.

STAR HANDS

My story by Gemma Howorth

When I was growing up, people would comment on how attractive my hands were. It was weird really, and I didn't take much notice. Then my friend's mother, a professional photographer, said to me, 'Seriously Gemma, your hands are better than all the girls I work with. You could be a professional hand model.' So I decided to give it a try!

I started hand modelling nine years ago, and set up my own model agency, Body London, in 2008. The agency specialised in modelling particular parts of the body, such as lips, hands and feet. Sometimes, I worked five or six days a week – a TV advertisement chopping carrots for a supermarket chain one day, and appearing on the fashion pages of *Vogue* the next.

Every time you've seen a supermodel in a photograph with a hand on her face – 99.9 per cent of the time, that hand will have been a hand model's. I've worked with Kate Moss quite a few times, with Lily Cole for Rimmel, and with Hollywood actress Rose Byrne for Max Factor. I had to lie on top of Rose for four hours with my little finger in her mouth! You wouldn't believe the jobs that I've done!

I've gone to extraordinary lengths to protect my hands. If I get a paper cut, I may be unable to work for two weeks. Whenever I cook, I wear a pair of washing-up gloves, sometimes two, to avoid burns, and I always moisturise my hands 20 or 30 times a day. Almond oil is the best treatment to use because it moisturises the cuticles, too.

The work for body part models seems to keep increasing. Hand models are by far the busiest – with all the new smart phones and tablet computers, hands are needed to show the size of a product, and demonstrate how it works. After hands, I'd say it was legs, feet, lips and eyes in that order.
It really does make you think about modelling in a whole new light!

Gemma Howorth
-x-

MOST SUCCESSFUL MODELS

These ladies are the reigning stars of the fashion industry – from billboards to magazine covers, they've done it all.

1. Gisele Bündchen

Currently the most successful model in the world, with an estimated income of US$45m (£29m) in 2010. Gisele grew up in the small Brazilian town of Três de Maio and at 14, visited São Paulo on a school trip. Here, she was spotted by Elite Model Management. Since then, she has worked with brands including Dolce & Gabbana, Dior and Versace and has appeared on over 600 magazine covers. By 30, Giselle had successfully launched her own range of sandals and beauty products.

2. Heidi Klum

With estimated earnings of US$20m (£13m) in 2010, Heidi is a major fashion success. She won a national modelling competition back home in Germany, before moving to New York to model full-time. She was the face of lingerie brand Victoria's Secret for 13 years, and since 2004 has presented the US reality show *Project Runway*. More recently, Heidi has launched a range of sportswear exclusively through Amazon.com.

3. Kate Moss

Britain's best-known supermodel, Kate earned an estimated £8.5m in 2010. At 14 years old, she was spotted by Sarah Doukas, the founder of Storm Model Management. By 18, she was appearing in advertisements for Calvin Klein, and flying backwards and forwards from London to New York up to eight times per week! In 2007, Kate began a partnership with Topshop in which she designed her own range of clothes. This deal reportedly earned her £1m per year.

4. Adriana Lima

At 15, Adriana won the prestigious Ford Models' 'Supermodel of Brazil' 1995 competition, and came second in the 'Supermodel of the World' in 1996. In 1999, she did her first fashion show for lingerie company Victoria's Secret. She was offered a contract in 2000 and has been working with them ever since. Additional contracts with Maybelline and Guess? earn Adriana an estimated US$8m (£5m) per year.

5. Naomi Campbell

At the age of 15, Naomi Campbell began modelling. At just 18, she became the first black woman to ever be featured on the cover of both French and British *Vogue*. She is said to be worth £48 million, but is most famous as the woman who paved the way for other models of colour to enter the world of fashion and catwalk modelling.

& GABBA

VITAL STATISTICS

£75

The standard editorial day rate for a *Vogue* shoot.

£29 MILLION

The estimated annual earnings of Brazilian supermodel Gisele Bündchen.

170

The number of countries showing the hit TV series *America's Next Top Model*. Includes Lithuania, Estonia and Taiwan.

£766,66.66

The amount of money Nicole Kidman earned per minute for a 2004 Chanel No. 5 TV advertisement!

1852

The year the world's first fashion model, the French model Maria Vernet Worth, appeared on a catwalk.

38-31-42

The stats of Crystal Renn, the world's most successful plus-size model. This makes her a UK dress size 16.

20 PER CENT

The standard commission that model agencies take from their models.

13

WORKING THE LOOK

From striking a pose in a magazine and looking larger than life on a billboard, to strutting their stuff down the catwalk, models work in a variety of different jobs.

On the page

Editorial work consists of photographs that appear in magazines. It is some of the lowest paid modelling work. However, the tear sheets, or pictures, that these shoots create are essential for a model's portfolio.

Perfect fit

In catalogues, models wear every outfit in a store's collection. For high street stores, showing their clothes worn by models, rather than just hanging on racks, is a huge boost to sales.

Ruling the runway

Catwalk modelling is the most demanding modelling work. Fashion designers require a specific look, and a catwalk model's career is short – typically models work between the ages of 16 and 25.

Going global

Advertising is the best-paid work a model can do, especially TV commercials (known as TVCs). The model is paid a day rate for the work and is then given a series of further payments to allow the company to use the images or advertisement in different countries. One day's work can end up being worth hundreds of thousands of pounds if an advertisement runs for a few years around the world. It is the modelling equivalent of winning the lottery!

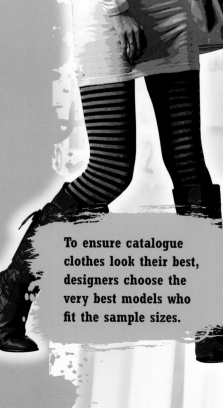

To ensure catalogue clothes look their best, designers choose the very best models who fit the sample sizes.

Editorial work requires models to adapt to several different looks and work with many photographers.

Celebrities, such as actress Eva Longoria now attract highly-paid advertising work.

Catwalk models are taller than most editorial and commercial models — around 178 centimetres for women and 185 centimetres for men.

MODEL SPEAK

Walk the walk and talk the talk with the Radar guide to modelling!

BMI (body mass index)
a way of estimating the percentage of a person's body fat by dividing his or her weight by the height multiplied by itself

book
slang for a portfolio

casting
an appointment to meet a magazine or company to assess a model's suitability for a specific job

catwalk show
an event where a fashion designer shows new clothes. Models walk on a catwalk so the audience can see the clothes from all angles

collection
the clothes that a designer has made for a specific event or period of time, for example a spring/summer collection or an autumn/winter collection

commercial
a type of modelling targeted at selling high street clothes or products, rather than fashion products

commission
the amount of money paid to an agent for finding work for a model

editorial
a magazine's fashion pages, rather than advertisements

fashion week
a series of fashion shows that take place in a particular fashion capital, such as London (UK), Paris (France), New York (USA) and Milan (Italy), to showcase new collections

go-sees
the visits models make to a potential client or photographer in order to get work

high fashion
the high-quality clothes made by top fashion designers

photoshoot
when a photographer takes pictures of a model for publication in a magazine or for use in an advertisement

Catwalk models jet-set around the world to appear at fashion shows during fashion weeks.

plus-size model
a model who is a UK dress size 14 or bigger

portfolio
the portfolio of photographs that a model takes to go-sees. It shows a range of looks and the style of work they can do

runway
another word for a catwalk. It resembles an airport runway, because it is long and straight

samples
clothes produced by fashion companies that are given to magazines before their new ranges go on sale so that they can publicise new designs. Samples are tailored to fit fashion models

tear sheets
a model's published work that has appeared in magazines

Vogue editor Anna Wintour is often seen in the front rows at major catwalk shows.

GLOSSARY

adrenalin
a hormone found in the human body that causes the heart to beat faster

annual earnings
the total amount of money that someone earns in one year

anorexia nervosa
an illness where a person becomes obsessed with losing weight by not eating

billboard
a large outdoor board used to display advertisements

body image
the perception a person has of themselves when they look in a mirror

bulimia
an eating disorder in which people often overeat and then make themselves sick

cuticles
the skin around a person's fingernails

debut
a first appearance

discrimination
unfair treatment of someone because of their race, age, sex or size, for example

negotiating
agreeing something through discussion

stats
short for statistics. In modelling, these are a model's measurements (height, chest, waist and hips)

JOY FATOYINBO

Joy grew up in Hamburg, Germany. He has worked for high-street brands Ikea, Debenhams and Mini Cooper among others. Here, he talks about life as a commercial model.

When did you start modelling?

I started at 23, which is very late! I was working in a bar in Berlin, and the owner, who was a photographer, took some pictures of me to advertise the bar. A friend put me in touch with a model agency, and they took me on.

What were you doing before?

I was training to be a lawyer. Even after graduating from university there are several more years training, so I used my earnings from modelling to help fund my studies. I also managed to find work placements in cities such as Paris, France and Cape Town, South Africa, which had busy modelling scenes so I could combine my two passions!

Is there a secret to being successful at castings?

I wish there was! Your portfolio is very important – it's the centre of your career so it needs to be kept up-to-date and have a good variety of images. A casting is like a job interview, so try to leave a good impression and make them remember you.

How do you feel when you don't get booked?

You can't take it personally. A lot of models find it hard to cope with rejection – but you have to realise that your face doesn't fit every job you try for.

How do you look after yourself?

I go to the gym three times a week. It's hard because I'm a naturally lazy guy, so I have to drag myself there! I try to eat well and avoid desserts. And I try to get plenty of sleep, particularly the night before jobs and important castings.

What will you do when you retire from modelling?

I'll go back to law and set up my own legal practice. I'd say to anyone thinking of modelling, always have a fall back. An education is very important.

HOLLYWOOD MODELS

Everywhere you look, there's a magazine or a billboard advertising a fashion brand or fragrance with the face of a well-known celebrity. How did the trend start and does it really work?

Instant recall

To keep sales healthy, companies need people to recognise and remember their product. Millions of pounds are spent creating this 'brand awareness' to encourage shoppers to choose one product over another. Celebrities have been a boost to product sales for years.

Scientists claim that seeing a celebrity in an advertisement can alter our thoughts, making us more likely to remember and buy that product. Fifties actress Marilyn Monroe is credited as the first 'celebrity model'. She was once asked what she wore to bed, and replied, 'Chanel No. 5, of course.' The celebrity model was born!

Celebrities take over

Most mainstream model agencies today have a special bookings section for the celebrities they represent. For example, Premier Model Management has a host of well-known faces on their books, from Nicky Hilton to actress Lucy Liu. It has

Liv Tyler is the face of cosmetic giant Givenchy. Singer Beyoncé Knowles promotes products for a number of companies including L'Oréal, Pepsi and Nintendo.

also become common to see celebrities promoting several brands at once.

Working on the team

As more brands use famous faces, companies have to dream up new ways of making an impact. A recent trend has seen celebrities working for the companies they represent. Camera company Polaroid made pop star Lady Gaga a creative director last year, and Black Eyed Peas front man Will.i.am is 'director of creative innovation' for computer chip maker Intel. This way, you not only get to use a celebrity's image, but can also tap into the creativity that made them famous in the first place.

TYSON BECKFORD

THE STATS

Name: Tyson Craig Beckford
Date of birth: 19 December 1970
Place of birth: New York, USA
Job: Model, actor, TV presenter

School days

Beckford was born in New York to a Jamaican father and a Chinese-Jamaican mother. His mother was a part-time fashion model, who often took him along to castings or to sit backstage when she had catwalk shows. At high school, Beckford enjoyed athletics and American football, but after leaving school he had a series of jobs and hoped to one day become an actor.

Spotted in the park

In the summer of 1991, a writer for hip-hop magazine *The Source* spotted Beckford playing football in a New York park. He was asked to model for the publication. From there, Beckford got himself a model agent and started shooting his first fashion assignments for the *The New York Times, GQ* and Marks and Spencer.

Making it big

No one could have predicted what came next. In 1993, fashion icon Ralph Lauren chose Beckford as the face of his Polo line of male sportswear. He was the first black male model to feature in the company's advertising. The campaign was a huge success, and Beckford soon signed an exclusive two-year deal with the brand. Beckford was named 'Man of the Year' by music channel VH1, and one of the '50 Most Beautiful People in the World' by *People* magazine. Campaigns with Gucci and Calvin Klein followed and Beckford became the world's first male supermodel.

Face for film

In recent years, Beckford has spread his wings into TV presenting, acting and producing. He has hosted the US reality show *Make Me A Supermodel* and made appearances in several movies, including the modelling comedy *Zoolander* (2001), with actor Ben Stiller. He has also helped to produce films including, *Kings of the Evening* (2008) and *Hotel California* (2008). Beckford may have retired from modelling, but his film work both on- and off-screen shows that he still loves the camera – and it still loves him!

BRAG

40th Annual Scholarship & Awards Gala

SIZE ZERO ON THE CATWALK – YES OR NO?

YES

The fashion industry has been criticised for using female models who look underweight to advertise clothes. They are known as 'size zero' models. Designers say:

1. The models they use might look thin, but most are all fit and well and have a body mass index of 18 or more, which is considered healthy.

2. Designers prefer to see tall, thin models wearing their clothes on the catwalk because they believe that they look better on slim models. Designers also believe the public prefer to see clothes on slim models.

3. It is hard to impose minimum measurements on models' sizes without being accused of discrimination. What about thin people, should they not be represented, too?

4. Ultra-thin models make up only around ten per cent of the fashion industry, and are used mainly for catwalk shows. The fashion industry should not be criticised for this small number of models, just because they are in the public eye more often than other types of models.

5. The industry is already doing a lot to promote diversity on the catwalk. In 2009, New York Fashion Week hosted its first show of plus-size clothes, and London Fashion Week presented older and plus-size models.

Critics say that size zero models should be replaced. They argue that:

1. Girls and women will be encouraged to aim for weight loss and a body shape that is unachievable and unhealthy.
2. Successful plus-size models such as Crystal Renn and Robyn Lawley are better role models for young women. The average UK women's dress size is 16 and models who are of a similar weight should represent them.
3. Maintaining a size zero shape can be extremely dangerous. Several fashion models have died because of health complications related to drastic dieting and eating disorders such as anorexia nervosa and bulimia.
4. Fashion magazines are forced to keep using size zero models because they are the only models who can fit into the clothes sent by designers to be used for photoshoots. Designers should make clothes for 'normal-sized' models and women.
5. The catwalk should reflect the diversity shown in the street – tall and short, big and small, young and old. There should not be just one narrow view of what makes someone attractive.

NO

YES OR NO?

Designers argue that taller and thinner models make their clothes look better, and so help them to sell their collections. Historically, tall, slender models have been used to model clothes for that reason. However, when young women compare themselves to models who are seriously underweight they may develop a negative body image and as a result try to drop to an unhealthy weight. Models should always be healthy, and no one's life should be put at risk to follow fashion.

SCARLETT JOHANSSON

The face the camera loves

THE STATS

Name: Scarlett Johansson

Date of birth: 22 November 1984

Place of birth: New York City, USA

Lives: Los Angeles, USA

Job: Actress, model

A Calvin Klein spokesman described Scarlett's advertising appeal as '...hip, fresh, with an urban sophistication'.

Child actress

The daughter of a Danish-born architect father and a film producer mother, Scarlett began acting when she was very young. She made her film debut at just nine years old and had memorable roles in the comedy *Home Alone 3* at 13 and *The Horse Whisperer* with movie icon Robert Redford at 14. Her breakthrough role came in 2003 in *Lost in Translation*, for which she won a BAFTA and was nominated for a Golden Globe award.

Face of the moment

Johansson's on-screen success has led to off-screen opportunities. Her first big modelling break came in 2004, when the then 19-year-old actress was offered a two-year contract by Calvin Klein as the face of a new fragrance, starring in print and TV advertisements. In 2006, she signed a deal worth US$4m (£2.5m) to be the face of cosmetics brand L'Oréal for a series of TV advertisements.

High fashion to high street

More modelling followed, with famous luxury brand Louis Vuitton booking Johansson for two ad campaigns in 2007 for their spring/summer and autumn/winter ranges. She also featured in Reebok's worldwide advertising campaign the same year.

The high street sportswear giant also tapped into Johansson's creative talents by hiring the actress to help them create a range of 'athletic-inspired footwear and clothing'.

Role perfect

Johansson's profile as an actress and model shows no signs of falling. Movie producers have recently decided she has the talents required for crowd-pleasing action roles. In 2010, she starred with Robert Downey Jr. in *Iron Man 2* and she featured in *The Avengers* in 2012. The fashion world needs no convincing that she has the look and style to help sell their products. In 2011, Johansson appeared in her third ad campaign for Dolce & Gabbana's make-up range, and her fourth campaign for fashion band Mango (she has been working with both brands since 2009). Model/actress, or actress/model, Johansson plays both roles perfectly.

Career highlights

1994 made her film debut at nine years old in comedy *North*

2003 won a BAFTA for her role in *Lost in Translation*

2006 appeared in TV ads for L'Oréal cosmetics

2009 named as the face of high street fashion brand Mango, and Dolce & Gabbana's make-up collection

2012 starred in comic book blockbuster *The Avengers* as Natasha Romanoff

FRONT ROW

Fashion shows are where designers introduce their new ranges...usually with some added glitz and sparkle!

The front row of a major fashion show is usually full of top fashion magazine editors and Hollywood A-listers. When Donatella Versace launched a collection for high street store H&M in 2011, she attracted actresses Uma Thurman, Blake Lively and Jessica Alba. Film director Sophia Coppola and supermodels Helena Christensen and Linda Evangelista were also in the audience!

In recent years, catwalk shows have become more than just fashion events. Many have become live concerts! Famous DJs or singers are often paid to perform, and fashion designers expect to spend up to £500,000 on a well-produced catwalk show.

Designers very carefully select which outfits will be shown on the catwalk and in what order. They expect fashion editors to examine the look and style of their clothes, and to appreciate the cut and the quality of each garment.

Paris Fashion Week is held in the Carrousel du Louvre, an underground shopping centre in the city. London's current venue for most of its Fashion Week's events is historic Somerset House. A large marquee is set up in the courtyard of the venue to hold shows from all the major designers. There are also one-off events and parties spread around the city!

Models are carefully selected for each fashion show, and if a new model is lucky enough to catch the eye of a major designer, it can launch their career. Fashion models are chosen for how well sample size clothes fit them, but also for their presence on the catwalk. Many top models have to master 'the walk' before they can become a success on the runway.

The fashion calendar revolve around major fashion shows London, Milan, Paris and Ne (shown here). Each city hos Fashion Weeks every year. recently, important events h sprung up in Seoul, Toyko, Angeles, Hong Kong, Buen Aires and Singapore.

EXIT

ACTION FIGURES

Models work in a record-breaking business – get the biggest, strangest and most extreme stats in this larger-than-life world!

Sky-high model

Who: Amazon Eve
When: 2011
Where: Beverly Hills, California, USA
What: World's tallest professional model
How: This personal-trainer-turned-model entered the record books in February 2011, when she measured 201.66 centimetres

Keep walking!

Who: Copenhagen Fashion Week
When: 2010
Where: Copenhagen, Denmark
What: World's longest catwalk
How: Organisers of Copenhagen's Fashion Week entered the record books by turning a popular shopping street into their show's catwalk. Unlike a typical catwalk, which is 7 metres long, the street is 1,609 metres long!

Jetsetter!

Who: Anja Rubik
When: 2010–11
Where: Everywhere!
What: World's most in-demand model
How: Polish catwalk model Anja Rubik was ranked the busiest model in the world – appearing on 59 magazine covers, and on 43 catwalks worldwide in a 12-month period

Going underground

Who: Berlin Fashion Week
When: 2006–present
Where: Berlin, Germany
What: World's only underground train catwalk
How: Every year during Berlin Fashion Week, models for 20 different designers strut their stuff on the Berlin Underground for invited audiences as trains do circuits of the city

Crowded catwalk

Who: EXPRESS fashion show
When: 2011
Where: New York City, USA
What: Most models on a catwalk
How: US clothing brand EXPRESS entered the Guinness World Records when 1,243 models walked down a runway in Times Square, New York, USA

Great brand loyalty

Who: Christie Brinkley
When: 1976–present
Where: Los Angeles, USA
What: Longest modelling contract with one company
How: US supermodel Brinkley became the face of CoverGirl cosmetics in 1976, and stayed with the company for almost 30 years until she resigned in 2005

Modelling pensioner

Who: Carmen Dell'Orefice
When: 2011
Where: New York City, USA
What: Oldest working model
How: American model Dell'Orefice celebrated her 80th birthday – and 66 years in the modelling industry! She first appeared on the cover of Vogue when she was 15

WALK THIS WAY!

If you want to be the face of the future, here are some brilliant ways to find out more about the career of your dreams!

Surf the net

There are some fantastic model sites to explore. Catwalk this way to some of the world's biggest model agencies!

IMG Models
Find out more about the world's number one agency, and home of supermodels Gisele Bündchen, Tyra Banks, Heidi Klum and Kate Moss:
www.imgmodels.com

Premier Model Management
Discover the UK's biggest model agency, recently featured in the TV series *The Model Agency*:
www.premiermodelmanagement.com

Reads & Apps

Professional Modelling by Louise Cole and Giles Vickers-Jones (New Holland Publishers, 2009)

The Teen Vogue Handbook: An Insider's Guide to Careers In Fashion (Puffin, 2010)

Follow the Model: Miss J's Guide to Unleashing Presence, Poise, and Power by J. Alexander (Gallery Press, 2010)

The TV series *Britain's Next Top Model* offers free podcasts after every episode, including interviews with contestants. Available on iTunes:
www.itunes.com

INDEX

advertising work 8, 11, 13 14–15, 18, 21, 23, 24, 26–27
body part models 8–9
bookers 7, 19, 21
castings 6–7, 19, 22

catalogue work 14, 23
catwalk shows 4–5, 11, 13, 14–15, 22, 24–25, 28–29, 30–31
celebrity models 15, 20–21, 26–27
editorial work 12, 14–15
fashion week 24, 29, 30

go-sees 6
model agencies 7, 8, 10–11, 13, 18, 21
plus-size models 13, 24–25
portfolios 14, 19
scouts 7, 10–11, 23
size zero models 24–25

Get more hot topic reads!

Celebrity Make-up Artist
Celebrity Stylist
Being a Celebrity Photographer

Ice Dancing
Latin Dance

Street Dance
Bhangra & Bollywood
Capoeira

The Armed Services
The Special Forces
Undercover Operations
Police Forensics

Are you on the Radar?